What lies on the ground, one hundred feet in the air?
A dead centipede.

"If Abraham Lincoln were alive today," said the teacher, "what would he find that he was most famous for?"
Ricky raised his hand and answered "Old age."

What do you call people who keep a calculator in their trouser pocket?
Smarty pants.

Standing at the train station, Wilson asked Woodrow, "Does this train run on time?"
"No," said Woodrow. "It runs on the track."

What kind of computers are the friendliest?
The ones with good relation-chips.

500
Hilarious Jokes
for Kids

Jeff Rovin

A SIGNET BOOK

SIGNET
Published by New American Library, a division of
Penguin Group (USA) Inc., 375 Hudson Street,
New York, New York 10014, USA
Penguin Group (Canada), 90 Eglinton Avenue East, Suite 700, Toronto,
Ontario M4P 2Y3, Canada (a division of Pearson Penguin Canada Inc.)
Penguin Books Ltd., 80 Strand, London WC2R 0RL, England
Penguin Ireland, 25 St. Stephen's Green, Dublin 2,
Ireland (a division of Penguin Books Ltd.)
Penguin Group (Australia), 250 Camberwell Road, Camberwell, Victoria 3124,
Australia (a division of Pearson Australia Group Pty. Ltd.)
Penguin Books India Pvt. Ltd., 11 Community Centre, Panchsheel Park,
New Delhi - 110 017, India
Penguin Group (NZ), 67 Apollo Drive, Rosedale, North Shore 0632,
New Zealand (a division of Pearson New Zealand Ltd.)
Penguin Books (South Africa) (Pty.) Ltd., 24 Sturdee Avenue,
Rosebank, Johannesburg 2196, South Africa

Penguin Books Ltd., Registered Offices:
80 Strand, London WC2R 0RL, England

First published by Signet, an imprint of New American Library,
a division of Penguin Group (USA) Inc.

First Printing, May 1990
30 29 28 27 26 25 24 23 22

Copyright © Jeff Rovin, 2002
All rights reserved

Ⓓ REGISTERED TRADEMARK—MARCA REGISTRADA

Printed in the United States of America

ACKNOWLEDGMENTS

Special thanks to Adam Heaton, Ryan Quirk, Nate Sheldon, Matt Dunn, Brendan Begnal, and most of all to Sam Rovin.

INTRODUCTION

Here's a question for you: what can be found between soft covers and makes you laugh?

Answer: a clown in your bed!

Another answer, of course, is this book!

What makes *500 Hilarious Jokes for Kids* so special?

For one thing, it contains many, many jokes you've never heard anywhere. Not only will they give you a chuckle, but you'll have brand-new jokes to tell your friends!

For another thing, the jokes are grouped by topics. If you want to find a joke about a dog or a bug or a pig, just turn to the category of ANIMALS. Or go to SCHOOL and you'll find everything from rotten students to silly teachers. In GHOSTS AND MONSTERS, there are creatures ranging from vampires to zombies to Godzilla and King Kong. Want a gag about football? Baseball? Boxing? Bowling? Take a gander at the chapter on SPORTS.

We've also got KNOCK KNOCK jokes, rib-ticklers about PARENTS, gags about BRATTY KIDS, and many more. And in the GRAB BAG section, you'll find jokes that didn't fit into the other categories . . . but were just too good to leave out.

For you fans of really disgusto jokes, take a peek at the YUCCH! category, where we introduce the truly sickening Jimmy the Bug-Eater. After reading this section, we promise you'll never even *look* at a worm again.

Here's another question for you: what's black and white and red all over?

Answer: a sunburned penguin. But we also think this book is a good good answer, for it's sure to be read over and over!

BRATTY KIDS

The *very* fat lady stopped on the curb and said to the boy, "Young man, could you see me across the road?"

"Across the road?" said the kid. "Lady, I could see you when you were still a block away!"

Bratty Bob was running through the neighbor's garden.

"Hey!" shouted the neighbor. "I told you not to let me catch you there again!"

"Right!" said the boy. "And you haven't caught me yet!"

Freddie walked into the house crying.

"What's wrong?" asked his grandmother.

"I just lost a quarter!"

"There, there," said his grandmother. "Here's another."

As soon as the woman gave Freddie a new quarter, he began crying even louder.

"Now what's wrong?" his grandmother asked.

"I wish I said a lost a dollar!"

"Hey, Ma," said Rufus, "can I have fifty cents to stop a guy from crying in the street?"

"Why, of course," said his mother. "That's very thoughtful of you. What's he crying?"

" 'Ice cream, fifty cents!' "

"Guess what I found out?" tough little Arthur said to his friend. "You know what's more fun than watching the cuckoo pop out of a cuckoo clock?"

"No, what?"

"Watching your grandfather pop out of the grandfather clock!"

There was a metal bucket in the backyard, and bratty Bart was banging it.

"Just what do you think you're doing?" his father yelled.

"Making music for the new baby," Bart said.

"Don't lie to me! The baby isn't out here."

"Sure she is," said Bart. "She's inside the bucket!"

Mrs. Morgan came over and gave her son a kiss.

"That was very nice of you to let your sister borrow your skates to go on the lake."

"Sure, Ma. How else was I going to find out if the ice was thick enough?"

"Why are you so late getting home?" Mrs. Smith asked her son Duke.

"I stopped two kids from fighting."

"That was very nice," she said. "How did you do that?"

Duke shrugged. "I beat them both up."

"Where are you hiding, Tony?" Mr. Denham yelled. "I'll teach you to eat all your sister's candy!"

"It's okay!" Tony cried. "I already know how to do it!"

Isaac walked into the house, his pants soaking wet.

"Oh, dear!" his mother wailed. "What happened?"

"I fell into a puddle."

"In your new trousers?"

"Sorry, Mom." Isaac said, "but I didn't have time to change while I was falling."

"Who broke the window?" Mr. Wilson demanded to know.

"My brother," said pesky little Dennis.

"How did he do that?"

"He ducked when I threw a stick at him!"

12

Nasty Ned said to his classmate Jed, "I bet I can make you say white."

"And I bet you can't," said Jed.

"Okay. What color is the sky?"

"Blue."

"And what color is blood?"

"Red."

"You see?"

"See what?" Jed asked. "You said you'd make me say *white*."

Ned smiled. "There. You just did "

Nasty Ned still wasn't finished. He said to his rich classmate Blair, "I bet I have more money in my pocket than you have."

Blair accepted the bet. Ned emptied his pocket and counted what he had: it was only sixty cents. Blair emptied her pocket: she had four dollars.

"I win!" she said.

"No," said Ned. "I won."

"But four dollars is more than sixty cents!" she said.

"I know," said Ned, "but we bet who had more money in *my* pocket."

When Nasty Ned came home, he said to his younger sister, "When I was born, they passed out the champagne."

"What happened when I was born?" his sister asked.

"They just passed out."

Cybill said to Bruce, "You want to come to my birthday party on Saturday?"

"Sure. Where do you live?"

"I'm at 32 Oak Ridge Road. When you get there, ring the doorbell with your nose."

"Why with my nose?" asked Bruce.

"Because," said Cybill, "your hands better be full of presents!"

Rotten Roger said to Marv, "Let's see who can say the alphabet the fastest!"

Marv agreed, and said, "A, B, C, D, E—"

Meanwhile, Roger said, "The alphabet! I win!"

Crumby Cynthia said to her classmate, "Bet you a dollar I can spell scrambled eggs with just four letters."

When her classmate agreed to the bet, Cynthia said, "G-s-e-g."

Cynthia asked another classmate, "What's the difference between snow and snew?"

"What's snew?"

Cynthia said, "I don't know. What's new with you?"

Bratty Brenda said to Waldo, "Your ideas are like comets."

"You mean, they're very bright?"

"No," she said. "They're very rare."

Brenda made Waldo a bet.

"I bet I can spell '80' with just two letters."

"You're on," said Waldo.

After they put their money on the table, Brenda smiled and said. "A-T."

CLOTHING

Q: Why does underwear last longer than all other clothing?

A: Because it's never worn out.

Little David came downstairs one morning, crying.

"What's wrong?" his father asked.

"My feet hurt!" the boy wailed.

His father looked at them and smiled. "Well, that's because you have your shoes on the wrong feet!"

The boy cried even louder. "Then what am I going to do? I don't have any other feet!"

Q: What's the only coat you put on wet?
A: A coat of paint.

Q: What kind of pants did Mr. Van Winkle wear?
A: Dungarees with a Rip in them.

Q: What kind of clothing does a house wear?
A: Address.

Q: What's the difference between a gardener and a clothes cleaner?
A: One gets the lawn wet, the other gets the laun-dry.

Q: Where can you find the nearest army?
A: Up your sleevy.

Q: What did the torn sock say to the shoe?
A: "Well, I'll be darned!"

Q: Why did the man go crazy in the clothing shop?
A: He was told it was a good place for a fit.

Q: What do you call people who keep a calculator in their trouser pocket?
A: Smarty pants.

Q: What country is the best place on Earth to shop for neckwear?
A: Thailand.

Lum walked up to Abner.

"Say, Abner, do you have holes in your socks?"

"Heck, no!"

"Really?" said Lum. "Then how do you get your feet into them?"

Mr. DiFate walked into the clothing store and dropped a bundle of clothing on the table.

"These pants are too tight!" he complained.

"But I altered them myself!" protested the tailor. "They should fit you like a glove."

"They do. Now loosen them so they fit me like trousers!"

Mrs. Kaplan said, "Whenever I'm down in the dumps, I buy myself a new hat."

"Ah," said Mrs. Wengler. "So *that's* where you get them!"

Mr. Johnson and Mr. Kennedy were on a business trip together.

"Say—where'd my shoes go?" Mr. Johnson asked.

"Search me."

"Don't be silly. Where would you hide my shoes?"

The new shoemaker asked his boss, "What kind of fabric makes the best sneakers?"

"I don't know, but I can tell you what makes the best slippers."

"What?" asked the new shoemaker.

"Banana peels."

Q: What happens when a man wears his shoes out?

A: He wears them back inside again.

Q: What do germs wear after taking a bath?

A: A mic-robe.

Q: How are a hillbilly boy and an Eskimo alike?

A: One wears no shoes, the other wears snowshoes.

COMIC BOOKS AND COMIC STRIPS

"Say," Superdude said to Mighty Fellow, "I hear Mr. Amazing got into trouble last night."

"Yeah," said Mighty Fellow, "he sure did."

"What was the problem?"

"He threw a party."

"So?" said Superdude. "What's wrong with that?"

Mighty Fellow replied. "He threw it all the way to Mars!"

Waking up one morning, the Incredible Bulk entered a grocery store and began eating everything in sight, including the freezers, counters, and lights.

A brave clerk walked over to him.

"You know, Mr. Bulk, I'll bet there are two things you can't have for breakfast."

"You lie!" the big hero replied. "Bulk eat anything!"

"Nope," said the clerk.

The Bulk stopped. "Okay. What two things can Bulk not eat for breakfast!"

The clerk said, "Lunch and supper."

After watching Amazing Lady on television, Sally said to her friend Toby, "I'm pretty amazing, too. I can jump higher than this house."

"Bet you a quarter you can't!" Toby said.

They shook on the bet, then went outside. Crouching down, Sally jumped into the air . . . and went a foot off the ground.

"Ha!" said Toby. "You didn't jump higher than the house."

"Sure I did!" said Sally, grabbing the quarters. "The house didn't jump at all!"

Q: Why did Charlie Brown decide to leave his comic strip?

A: He was sick and tired of working for Peanuts.

Q: What do you call a superhero who won't let you borrow his toys?
A: Bratman.

Q: What's the name of the superhero who turns red faster than anyone else?
A: The Flush.

Q: What's the name of the super-fast tuna?
A: The Flish.

Q: What's the name of the superhero who loves clam chowder?
A: Souperman.

Q: What's the name of the superhero who loves ice cream?
A: Scooperman.

Q: What's the name of the nosy superhero?
A: Snooperman

"Did you ever wonder where comic-strip characters get their names?" Meg asked Annie

"No. By the way, my mom said we can have ice cream while she's gone. Do you want a lot at once, or a bit at a time."

Meg said, "I'd like a little, often, Annie."

Q: What would have happened if a radio-active spider had bitten Mr. Ed instead of Peter Parker?
A: The superhero would have been called Spider-mane.

Q: What if the spider had bitten a lunatic?
A: The superhero would have been Spider-maniac.

Q: What if the spider had bitten a dummy?
A: The superhero would have been Spider-mannequin.

Q: Like, why couldn't Alfred, the butler, play baseball?
A: Because he couldn't find the bat, man.

Q: Where does Batman go when he gets dirty?
A: Straight to the bat-tub.

Q: What mysterious rock from outer space causes Superman to become ugly for the evening?
A: Creep-tonite.

Q: What mysterious rock from outer space causes Superman to turn into a baby?
A: Crib-tonite.

Q: What song does Tarzan sing at Christmas?
A: "Jungle Bells."

Q: What song does the *Daily Planet* staff sing at Christmas?
A: "Perry White Christmas."

Q: What space hero would rather be home tending to his flowers?
A: Flash Garden.

"Wanna come with me to get a haircut, Ian?" asked young Roderick.

"Sure," said Ian. "Who does your hair?"

"The guy with the sword."

"Who cuts hair with a sword?"

Roderick said, "Conan the barber, Ian."

Q: Who is the most polite person on Eternia?
A: He-Manners.

Q: Who's the richest ghost in the comics?
A: Cash-per.

Q: What were Tarzan's last words?
A: Who greased the viiiiiiine . . . ?"

Q: What does Garfield eat for breakfast?
A: Mice Krispies.

Q: Who was the heaviest hero in the West?
A: Ton-to.

Q: What did they call Tonto's friend after he was mashed by a rolling boulder?
A: The Looooong Ranger.

Q: Why couldn't Batman start the Batmobile?
A: The bat-tery was dead.

Q: Why can't the Joker ever beat Batman?
A: Because Batman never loses a bat-tle.

Q: Where does the Man of Steel buy all of his food?

A: At a supermarket.

Q: Who fires silver bullets and is radioactive?

A: The Glowin' Ranger.

Q: Name the science-fiction hero who also plays hockey.

A: Puck Rogers.

Q: Name the science-fiction hero who never. ever gets into a spaceship without fastening his seat belt.

A: Buckle Rogers.

Q: What did they call the secret agent who dyed his hair?
A: James Blond.

Q: Where did James Bond go when he died?
A: To Double-O's Heaven.

Tarzan was tired when he walked into his hut.

"What have you been doing?" asked Jane.

"Chasing a herd of elephants on vines."

"Really?" said Jane. "I thought elephants stayed on the ground."

COMPUTERS AND VIDEOGAMES

"Sis," said the little boy, "would you bake me a videogame cake?"

"A videogame cake? How do you make that?"

The boy thought for a minute, then said, "I guess you use Ninten-dough."

The teacher knew that young Judd had been playing too many videogames! When she asked him to count as high as he could go, he said, "One, two, three, four, five, six, seven, eight, nine, ten, do!"

Q: What's the name of the police officer who makes sure that videogames aren't stolen from Nintendo factories?
A: Eliot NES.

Q: What's a videogame player's favorite outdoor activity?
A: Hide and Sega.

Q: What is a baby computer's first word?
A: "Da-ta."

Q: What do you call the factory where many computers are made?
A: Apple source.

Q: Why did the computer programmer get angry at her machine?
A: It gave her a little byte.

Q: Are computers fond of people?
A: You bet! People turn them on.

"I'm afraid," said the programmer, "my computer is dead."

"Gee, that's terrible," said a friend. "What did it die of?"

"A terminal illness."

The next day, the programmer went out and bought the same kind of computer.

"How's the new machine?" the friend asked.

"It's a microchip off the old block!"

Q: How does a computer feel when it's overworked?
A: Disk-gusted.

Q: What did the calculator say to the accountant?
A: "You can count on me!"

Q: What did the computers do when they fell in love?
A: They went on a data, of course.

Q: What kind of computer is deadly?
A: A poisonal computer.

Q: What kind of computers are the friendliest?
A: The ones with good relation-chips.

Q: What kind of animal feeds on computer circuits?
A: A chipmunk.

Q: Why was the computer sent to jail?
A: For executing a program.

Q: What's a computer's favorite game?
A: Cops and robots.

Every morning, Mrs. Schmidt went to work on her computer. And every morning, after breakfast, her young son Hans came over and touched the keys, covering them with peanut butter, jelly, or whatever else he had eaten.

Finally, the computer had enough. One morning, when Ms. Schmidt turned the computer on, this message appeared on the screen:

"I won't do anything until you take your dirty Hans off of me!"

Mr. Sculley walked up to the worker at the computer assembly plant.

"You're fired!" barked the boss.

"Why?" cried the worker. "I haven't done anything!"

"I know. That's why you're fired!"

Graham went for an interview at a computer company.

"You start by earning three hundred dollars a week," said the woman who interviewed him. "Then, in a year, you'll get five hundred a week."

"Great," said Graham, "I'll come back in a year."

"Do you type in data using one hand or both hands?" Ms. Curtis asked the new programmer.

"Neither," said the programmer. "I use the keyboard."

Q: What kind of sounds do clocks make in a Nintendo factory?

A: Joystick-tock, joystick-tock . . .

Q: How is the Abominable Snowman like a stolen Zelda cartridge?

A: They're both a Missing Link.

Q: What's a Nintendo fan's favorite drink?
A: Hawaiian Punch-out.

Q: How does a person's thumb feel after too many hours of videogaming?
A: Nintender.

"Morgan," said his father, "this report card is terrible. Didn't I promise to buy you Nintendo if you did well?"

"Yes, sir."

"Then why didn't you study?"

"Because," said Morgan, "I was too busy learning how to use my friend's Nintendo."

Q: What kind of music do computers like best?
A: Disk-o.

Q: Do computers have brothers?
A: No. Just tran-sisters.

Q: What kind of hardware do barbers use?
A: Comb-puters.

Q: What kind of hardware is used on the bottom of the sea?
A: Clam-puters.

Q: What kind of hardware do bakers use?
A: Crumb-puters.

Q: What did the programmer do when she found blades of grass growing from her disc drive?
A: She modem.

Q: What is a computer's favorite snack?
A: Silicon chips.

Q: What do you call a videogame that's been left too close to the radiator?
A: Hotari.

DINOSAURS

Q: What do you call a dinosaur that steps on everything in its way?
A: Tyrannosaurus Wrecks.

Q: What do you call a dinosaur that's never late?
A: A prontosaurus.

Q: What's big and fierce and is worn around your neck?
A: A tie-rannosaurus.

Q: What weighs ten tons, has a long neck, and goes "*ka-boom*"?
A: Dino-mite.

Q: What weighs ten tons, has a long neck, and cuts through wood?
A: A dino-saw.

Q: What did the plant-eating dinosaur say when winter ended and the trees sprouted new growth?
A: "Whew! That's a re-leaf!"

Q: What's as big as a dinosaur but doesn't weigh anything?
A: The dinosaur's shadow.

Q: What do you call a dinosaur who never gives up?
A: Try-ceratops.

Q: Who was the scariest dinosaur of them all?
A: The terror-dactyl.

Q: Who was the most famous actor in prehistoric times?
A: Mastodon Johnson.

Q: What do you call a dinosaur who's always walking in mud?
A: Brown-toe saurus.

Q: What prehistoric animal spent most of its time talking?
A: The woolly mam-mouth.

Q: What would you call a prehistoric skunk?
A: Ex-stinct.

Brian Braggart said to a classmate, "My dad is the best dinosaur hunter in the world!"

"Don't be ridiculous," the classmate replied. "There *are* no more dinosaurs."

Brian answered, "See how good my dad is?"

Miltie said to his friend Nellie. "Suppose you were in a prehistoric jungle and a tyrannosaurus attacked you. What would you do?"

"I'd run into a cave."

"Okay. Suppose you came out, and an allosaurus attacked you."

"I'd run into another cave."

"Fine. Suppose you came out of that one, and a gorgosaurus attacked you."

"I'd run into another cave."

"Now hold on," Miltie said. "Where are you getting all these caves from?"

Nellie replied, "The same place you're getting all these dinosaurs."

Q: What did the baby brontosaurus get when the daddy brontosaurus sneezed?
A: Out of the way!

Q: What did the manta ray become when the brontosaurus waded into the water and stepped on it?
A: An ex-ray.

Q: What kind of dinosaurs live in graveyards?
A: Cemetery-dactyls.

Q: What do you call a prehistoric animal the day after it's exercised much too much?
A: A dinosore.

Q: What's the difference between a world without prehistoric monsters and a room with no way out?
A: One has no dinosaurs, the other no sign o' doors.

Q: What should you do if a tyrannosaurus charges?

A: Take away its MasterCard.

DUMMIES

When he heard his friend calling from the bottom of a well, Joe ran over.

"Hey—how'd you get down there?" asked Joe.

"Dummy!" the friend said. "I took a little trip!"

While walking home from school, Bennie said to his friend Keith, "Did you know that a crescent moon is heavier than a full moon?"

"That's silly," Keith said. "The moon weighs the same all the time."

"Dummy!" Bennie said. "My teacher said the full moon is always lighter."

As they were walking down the street, a dummy said to his friend, "Boy, I sure hope this rain keeps up."

"Why?" said his friend.

"Because then it wouldn't come down."

A girl asked her dummy friend, "Which would you rather have happen: a building fall on you, or a car?"

After thinking for a moment, the dummy friend said, "I would rather have the building fall on a car."

While walking in front of an appliance store, the dummy saw a sign out front that said, "Iron Sinks."

Turning to a friend, the dummy said, "Of course it does! It's too heavy to float!"

Q: Why did the dummy stand in front of the mirror with her eyes shut?

A: So she could see what she looked like when she was asleep.

Every day, dumb Mr. Koch had to cross the river by ferry in order to get to work.

Waking up late one morning, he dressed quickly, ran out the door, and raced to the dock. The boat was several yards away, and stepping back and taking a mighty leap, Mr. Koch landed with a crash on the deck.

"Made it!" he cried triumphantly.

"So?" said one of the passengers, "What was the rush? This boat is coming in."

Q: Why did the dummy sleep in a vat of salad dressing?
A: So he'd be sure to get up very oily.

Mr. Griswald was staring at the cage in the zoo, watching the great cat pace back and forth.

"I wonder what that tiger would say if it could talk," he said to the zookeeper.

The zookeeper replied, "It would probably say, 'Hey, dummy, I'm a cheetah!' "

"My new watch is going to stop working any second," said Dumb David.

"How can you tell?" his friend asked.

"Just look!" said David, holding out the watch. "Its hours are numbered."

Carl said to Dumb Don. "When I was lost in the woods, I had to live on a can of peas for a whole week."

"That's amazing!" said Dumb Don. "Weren't you afraid you'd fall off?"

Mrs. Dimm said to her friend Mrs. Dumm, "My husband doesn't understand me at all. Does yours?"

"Why, Mrs. Dimm," said Mrs. Dumm, "I don't believe he's ever met you."

"Hey, Louie," said Marcel, "does your watch tell time?"

"No," said Louie. "You have to look at it."

"Well, what time is it?" Marcel asked Louie.

"Four o'clock."

"Isn't that amazing," said Marcel. "I've been asking people that same question all day, and everyone tells me something different!"

Q: Why did the dummy bring his bowling ball into the bathroom?
A: He wanted to see the toilet bowl.

Q: Why did an even bigger dummy bring Mike Tyson's gloves into the kitchen.
A: He wanted to see the cereal box.

Q: Why did the dummy's flying school fail?
A: Because she was only offering crash courses.

"Did you hear about the dummy who punched his clock?" Waldo asked his friend.

"No. Why?"

Waldo said, "The clock struck too!"

"How did the clock feel when it was punched?" the friend asked.

"What do you think?" asked Waldo. "Ticked off!"

Mrs. Dumdum walked into the bakery.

"Are these cookies tasty?" she asked.

"Oh, yes," said the baker. "They've been our most popular item for years."

"I see," said Mrs. Dumdum. "But I was hoping to get something baked more recently than that."

Mr. Nitwit arrived at the office, his head dripping with black gunk.

"What happened to you?" his boss asked.

"Oh," said Mr. Nitwit, "my alarm clock was broken, so I put grease in my hair."

"Why'd you do that?"

"I wanted to make sure I woke up oily."

Q: Why did the dummy eat a dollar?
A: Because when his mother gave it to him, she told him it was for lunch.

Q: Why did the dummy eat a candle?
A: He wanted a light meal.

"Guess what," said Mr. Nutso. "I dropped my clock in the river and it's still running."

"Wow," said his friend, "that's a tough clock."

"No," said Mr. Nutso, "I don't mean the clock is still running. I mean the river."

Q: Why did the dummy put candy on her pillow?
A: So she'd have sweet dreams.

"It was terrible," Mr. Dim said to a coworker. "I had to get up at four o'clock in the morning to answer the door in my pajamas."

"Gee," said the coworker. "I didn't know they made pajamas with doors."

"Can you stand on your head?" Lionel asked Dumb Dora.

"Don't be silly," Dora replied. "How could I get my feet all the way up there?"

"How would you like your hair cut?" the barber asked dopey Dennis.

"I'd like it cut off," Dennis replied.

Kooky Carol walked into the post office and said to the clerk, "If I put a stamp on this letter, will it go to my cousin in New York?"

"Yes, it will."

"That's too bad," Carol said. "I've addressed it to my friend in Boston."

"Gee, Mom," said Abner as they walked through the woods, "what are these holes in the trees?"

"They're knotholes."

"What do you mean they're not holes?" he asked. "I can see inside them!"

The new rancher called the local veterinarian.

"I don't understand it, doc. All of my cattle die while we're branding them."

"Hmmm . . . that is strange. I'd better come out and have a look. Which ranch is yours?"

"The Single-M, Double-O, Triple X, Circle W, Seven-Bar Nine-Y Ranch."

"And here," said the real-estate agent, "is a house without a single flaw."

"Really?" said the dumb home buyer. "Then what keeps you from falling into the basement?"

"You!" shouted the police officer as Dim Dinsdale crossed the street. "Didn't you see the 'Don't Walk' sign?"

"Sure," said Dinsdale. "I thought it was an ad for a bicycle store."

The dummy walked into a bank around noon.

"I'd like to see someone about borrowing money," she said to a teller.

"I'm sorry," said the teller, "but the loan arranger is out to lunch."

"Oh. Can I talk to Tonto, then?"

"Tell me, Katie," said Kathy, "do you ever have trouble making up your mind?"

"Yes and no."

Irving bumped into Simon on the street.

"Haven't I seen your face somewhere else?" asked Irving.

"I doubt it," said Simon. "It's always been attached to the rest of me."

One dummy said to the other, "Have you ever seen porpoises cry?"

"No," said the other, "but I've seen whales blubber."

"When's your birthday?" Mr. King asked Sam.

"August 24."

"What year?"

Sam replied, "Every year."

Two dummies were reading the newspaper ads, looking for work, when they found an ad for Tree Climbers.

"Gee," said one dummy, "too bad dere's only two of us."

Then there was the man who was so dumb that when he went to a mind reader, she was forced to give him his money back.

Q: Why did the dumb parents name both of their sons Ed?
A: Because they heard that two Eds are better than one.

The math teacher said, "Class, if there are three hundred and sixty-five days in a year, I want you to figure out how many seconds there are in a year."

Much to his disappointment, he had to give Dim Doug a zero, for Doug had written, "There are twelve. January 2, February 2, and so on, through December."

While Dumb Debbie was showing off her new magnifying glass, Mark said, "I see this magnifies things four times."

"Rats!" cries Debbie. "I've used it three times already!"

"I've lived on vegetables for my entire life," the young man said to Hortense. "What about you?"

"Oh," said Hortense, "I've lived on Main Street."

"Did you hear?" said witless Winnie. "The farm down the road isn't going to grow carrots any longer."

"Why not?"

"Because the farmer said the carrots are long enough!"

"Hey," said Fred, "this match won't light!"

"Strange," said Nutty Ned. "It worked okay this morning."

Standing at the train station, Wilson asked Woodrow, "Does this train run on time?"

"No," said Woodrow. "It runs on the track."

Dumb Dickie was walking through a museum of modern art. He stopped by one display and said to a guard, "I suppose this ugly, disgusting piece of horrible junk is called art."

"No, sir," said the guard, "You're looking at a mirror."

FICTIONAL CHARACTERS

Dr. Watson said to his friend Sherlock Holmes, "I've been meaning to ask you. What's your favorite kind of tree?"

"A lemon tree, my dear Watson."

Q: Where does Frosty the Snowman keep his money?
A: In a snowbank.

Q: Can Frosty see well in a blizzard?
A: Sure! He has terrific ice sight.

Q: Where does Frosty sleep?
A: On sheets of ice.

Q: Where does Frosty go when he wants to
   dance?
A: To a snow ball.

Q: Why is Frosty so popular?
A: Because he's cool!

A man ran up to a peasant and dropped a
bag of gold into his arm.

"What's this?" asked the peasant.

"It's gold! I'm Robin Hood! I rob from the
rich and give to the poor!"

"Hooray!" shouted the peasant. "I'm rich."

Robin Hood took out his sword. "In that
case, hand it over!"

Q: Whose nose grows when he tells a lie, is made of wood, and glows in the dark?
A: Pin-nuke-io.

Q: What do you get when you cross Christopher Robin's bear-friend with a skunk?
A: Winnie the p.u.

Q: Who was the lovely, storybook girl who placed her foot in a glass slipper . . . and smashed the slipper?
A: Cinder-elephant.

Q: Where does Santa Claus stay when he's away from the North Pole?
A: In a ho-ho-hotel.

Bambi ran into the deer camp, breathless.

"What's the matter?" asked his girlfriend Faline.

"A hunter with a bow came after me. Luckily, when he shot, he missed."

Faline said, "Sounds like an arrow escape!"

Q: Why did the basketball team place Cinderella on waivers?
A: Because she ran away from the ball.

Q: What did the movie dog Rin-Tin-Tin call his baby son?
A: Rin-Tin-Tinfant.

Q: Why was Lassie so smart?
A: She went to collie-age.

Q: What did Lassie get when she graduated?
A: Her dog-ree.

FOOD AND DRINK

"Care to join me in a cup of tea?" Mrs. Shanks asked when her friend Mrs. Prickley arrived at her home.

"Certainly," Mrs. Prickley replied, looking down at the cup. "But do you think we'll both fit?"

Q: Name something you can never have for lunch or dinner.
A: Breakfast.

Q: What kind of cookies do videogame players eat?
A: The kind made with Ninten-dough.

Q: What is a boxer's favorite beverage?
A: Punch.

Q: What is a 'fraidy cat's favorite food?
A: Chicken.

Q: What article of clothing can be made from banana peels?
A: Slippers.

Q: What breakfast cereal do you have when your pet bird flies into a fan?
A: Shredded tweet.

"Did you hear about the kid who ate sixteen griddle cakes for breakfast?" asked John.
"No!" said Sue. "How waffle!"

Q: Why was the cookie crying?
A: Because its mother had been a wafer so long.

Q: What happened when the student chef made a mess of an omelet in cooking school?
A: She was egg-spelled.

Q: Why were the oil and vinegar late for dinner?
A: Because they were dressing.

"Waiter!" screamed the man at the restaurant. "There's a bee in my soup!"

"Of course, sir," said the waiter. "It's alphabet soup."

"Waiter!" shouted the woman at the restaurant. "There's a rubber band in my soup!"

"Naturally," said the waiter. "You told me to bring you soup and make it snappy!"

"Waiter!" yelled another woman at the restaurant. "Will my hamburger be long?"

"No," said the waiter. "The hot dogs are long. The hamburgers are round."

Q: Why did the doughnut maker close her shop?
A: She was fed up with the hole business.

Q: What fruit is never lonely?
A: Pears.

Q: What do karate and judo experts eat before a workout?
A: Kung food.

Q: What famous author wrote poems about French Fries?
A: Edgar Allan Poe-tato.

Q: What famous author wrote plays about fruit?
A: William Shakes-pear.

Q: What branch of the military is only for fighting fruit?
A: The apple corps.

The customer stormed into the bakery.

"I want my money back!" the customer yelled. "This bread is full of holes!"

"Of course it is," said the baker. "It's hole-wheat bread."

Q: Where do super-smart frankfurters end up?
A: On an honor roll.

Lenny returned to the office after lunch and was stopped by Karen.

"Lenny—why do you have that hot dog in your shirt pocket?"

Lenny smacked his forehead. "Oh no! I must have eaten my pen for lunch!"

When they were cleaning up after the party, Ken said to his wife, "I think Anna hated your food."

"How do you know?"

"Oh," Ken said, "it came up during conversation."

"I've just invented the Food of Truth," Loree said to Donna. "One bite, and you immediately tell the truth."

Donna didn't believe her, but she dipped a fork into the slop and tasted some.

"Ecch!" snarled Donna. "That's dog food!"

"You see?" said Loree. "That's true!"

Before a romantic, candlelit dinner, Winston went to the store and asked for candles.

"Certainly," said the clerk. "Would you like them scented?"

"No," said Winston. "Put them in a bag and I'll take them now."

Q: What did Mary order when she went to the restaurant?

A: Mary had a little lamb.

Q: Why did the potato have a black eye?

A: It got in the way of the fruit punch.

Q: What did the little fruit use to shave itself?
A: A raisin blade.

Q: What's the worst kind of cake to have?
A: A stomachache.

A man walked into a restaurant.

"Do you serve crabs here?" he asked the hostess.

"Yes, sir," said the woman. "And we'll try to cheer you up."

"Waiter," said the customer, "there's no chicken in this chicken salad."

"Of course not, sir. You don't get a cat in cat food, do you?"

The teacher said to the cooking class. "Tell me: what is the most important thing to put in a chocolate cake?"

Faith quickly replied, "Your teeth!"

After correcting Faith, the cooking teacher said, "Who can tell me the best way to keep yogurt from spoiling?"

Faith answered, "By eating it."

A man walked into a restaurant. With him was a polar bear.

"Do you serve Eskimos?" the man asked the nervous waiter.

"C-certainly we d-do."

"Great," said the man. "I'll have lobster, and bring an Eskimo for my friend, here."

Gertrude's mother gave her a bottle of soda to share with her friend Hortense. The two girls sat on the curb, and Gertrude proceeded to drink the entire bottle.

"Hey!" said Hortense. "I thought we were each supposed to have half!"

"We were," said Gertrude. "But my half was on the bottom, and I had to drink yours to get to it."

"Waiter!" snarled the diner. "Why is my food mashed to a pulp?"

"Well, sir, when you ordered your meal, you told me to step on it."

One woman said to another, "Did you hear about the farmer who never had to water his potatoes?"

"Didn't they die?"

"No. He just planted onions all around them, and the onions made the potatoes' eyes water."

"Mama," said the baby corn, "where did I come from?"

The mama corn replied, "The stalk brought you."

The manager of the supermarket's vegetable department walked over to the new stock boy.

"Why did you put little bells on the scale?" the manager asked.

"Because," said the boy, "I wanted to jingle all the weigh."

"Waiter," said the woman, "I'd like spaghetti, please."

"With pleasure, madam."

"No," she said. "With meatballs."

"Hey!" the rude customer shouted at the waiter.

"Just a moment," the waiter replied.

"Hey!"

"Just a moment!"

"*Hey*, waiter!"

The waiter turned and said angrily, "We don't usually serve that, but in your case I'll make an exception!"

The American chef was visiting Spanish restaurants.

"How do dishes in American compare to the ones over here?" asked a Spanish cook.

The American replied, "If you drop them, they break just as easily."

Q: When the orange fell from the tree, why did it roll a little and then just stop?
A: It ran out of juice.

Q: Where's the best place to find out the exact weight of pie?
A: Somewhere over the rainbow . . . weigh a pie.

Q: What did the bored Coke bottles do for amusement?
A: They played "Follow the Liter."

Q: How do vegetables travel from field to field?
A: They take a taxi cabbage.

Q: What does a seven-foot-tall butcher weigh?
A: Meat.

GHOSTS AND MONSTERS

Q: How did the witch get around when her broomstick broke?
A: She witch-hiked, of course.

The nurse walked into the busy doctor's office and said, "Doctor, the Invisible Man is here."

"Sorry," the doctor replied, "I can't see him."

Bet you didn't know this: the turning point in the life of lonely, young Dr. Frankenstein came when his mother told him to go out and make some friends.

Q: Which side of a haunted house is the most frightening?

A: The inside.

Q: What happened when Dracula saw the deadly rays of the sun?

A: He shouted from delight.

Q: What did the Invisible Man call his mother and father?

A: Transparents.

Q: Who isn't afraid to deliver mail to skeletons?

A: The bony express.

Q: What did the rooster's ghost say every morning at sunrise?

A: Cock-a-doodle-*boo*!

Q: What is a skeleton's favorite instrument?
A: The trom*bone*.

Q: Why can't skeletons play music in church?
A: They have no organs.

Q: Why does Count Dracula gargle every night?
A: Because he has bat breath.

Q: What does Count Dracula say after biting someone's throat?
A: It's been nice gnawing you.

Q: What do you call two thousand pounds of bones?
A: A skele-ton.

Q: What's the difference between zombies and patched jeans?
A: Zombies are dead men, the jeans men-ded.

Q: Why didn't the skeleton go to the dance?
A: It had no body to go with.

Q: What's the first thing a witch does when she checks into a hotel?
A: Calls broom service.

Q: What animal will you never find in a haunted house?
A: A scaredy-cat.

Q: What did the one-eyed jack-o'-lantern wear over its bad eye?
A: A pumpkin patch.

Q: When do zombies go to sleep?
A: When they're dead-tired.

Q: What's the only time a ghost can build a snowman?
A: In the dead of winter.

Q: What kind of music do werewolves like the best?
A: Violence concertos.

"I'm in love with a witch," one vampire said to the other.

"Really?" said his friend. "What's so special about her?"

"Oh," said the love-stricken vampire, "she's always charming."

Q: What do you call a skeleton who won't do any work around the house?
A: Lazy bones.

Q: Why did the cyclops have to shut down his school?

A: He only had one pupil.

Q: What kind of dance do graverobbers enjoy?

A: A vaults.

One graverobber asked the other, "Say, how wide is this cemetery?"

Looking into the darkness, the other said, "It's a grave yard."

Q: What time is it when you're being chased by five hungry dinosaurs?

A: Five after one.

Q: Why doesn't the Invisible Man like to go to parties?

A: He has nobody to dance with.

After watching a science-fiction film, Johnny said to his friend, "What do you think would happen if your whole left side was disintegrated by a laser beam?"

Thinking for a moment, his friend Dick replied, "You'd be all right."

Q: What's the worst thing about eating Godzilla steaks?
A: The months of leftovers!

Q: What's the best way to take King Kong's temperature?
A: With a *verrrrry* long thermometer.

Q: Exactly how fast do you have to run to outrace the Wolfman?
A: One step faster than him!

While chasing the Amazing Colossal Man, the general stopped a motorist and said, "Is this the road the giant took?"

"No," said the motorist, "this road is still here."

Q: Why did Count Dracula flunk out of art school?
A: He could only draw blood.

"Ma," said the baby werewolf, "is it all right to eat vegetables with your fingers?"

"No," said the mother werewolf. "You eat the vegetables first, *then* you eat the fingers."

Q: What is the Lock Ness Monster's favorite meal?
A: Fish and ships.

Q: What's Count Dracula's favorite holiday?
A: Fangsgiving.

Coming home from work, Mrs. Dracula saw her son, Dracula Jr., chasing a man around the house.

"Junior!" she yelled. "How many times have I told you not to play with your food?"

Q: Why did the ghost become a cheerleader?
A: To add some team spirit.

"Guess who I'm defending?" one lawyer said to the other.

"Who?"

"The Blob. A farmer's suing the ooze monster for eating his dog."

"The Blob won't win the case," said the other lawyer.

"Why not?"

"Because he doesn't have a leg to stand on."

Q: What do vampires say when they kiss?
A: Ouch!

Q: What is Gorgo's favorite vegetable?
A: Squash.

Q: What is Gorgo's favorite sport?
A: Squash.

Q: After eating squash and playing squash, what does Gorgo drink to wash it down?
A: Crush.

Q: And what does Gorgo watch on TV while enjoying Crush?
A: "M*A*S*H."

Q: What happened when Dracula had a wrestling match with Hulk Hogan?

A: The Hulkster went down for the Count.

Q: Why did Godzilla eat Tokyo, pass by Rome, and then gobble down London?

A: He didn't want to eat between meals.

Q: What do you call a creature with three eyes, blue skin, five legs, and huge claws?

A: Extremely ugly.

Q: What do you get when you cross Count Dracula with someone who loves baseball?

A: A fanpire.

Q: What does a monster read to learn about its future?

A: A horror-scope.

Q: What would you get if you crossed the Invisible Man and a hippo?

A: A big nothing!

Q: What flavor shake does Dracula like the best?

A: Vein-illa.

Q: What kind of coffee does Dracula drink when he wakes up?

A: De-coffin-ated.

Q: What is the soft, gooshy stuff between King Kong's toes?

A: Slow natives.

Q: What's the best way to see flying saucers?

A: Trip the waiter.

Walking into his cave, Mr. Dragon looked at the armor scattered around. "Am I late for dinner?" he asked Mrs. Dragon.

"Yes," she said. "Everyone's eaten."

Q: What is Dracula's favorite sport?
A: Bat-minton.

Q: What inning is it when the Wolfmen take the field?
A: The fright-inning.

Q: How many monsters does it take to screw in a light bulb?
A: Ten. One to screw in the light bulb, and nine to rebuild the house.

Q: Where are the greatest dragons of all time honored?
A: In the Hall of Flame.

Q: What did they call the vampire who drank much too much blood?

A: Dracu-lard

Q: What time is it when Count Dracula climbs from his coffin?

A: Time to hide!

"Sorry," said the monster at the cemetery gate. "You can't come in here."

"But why not?" said the ghoul. "There's a party for ghouls going on, and I'm a ghoul."

"I know," said the monster at the gate, "but no one is allowed in without an engraved invitation."

Q: What does a witch say each night when she puts her broom away?

A: "Time to go to sweep."

Q: Where do ghosts go to get their hair done?
A: To a boo-ty parlor.

Q: What is a demon's favorite snack?
A: Devil Dogs.

Q: What kind of dog do most vampires own?
A: Bloodhounds.

Shecky and Becky were wandering in the desert.

"Tell me a ghost story," Shecky said.

"Why?" gasped Becky.

He replied, "Because they're so chilling."

Q: What kind of vegetables do ghouls like best?
A: Tomb-atoes.

Q: What do you call a mistake a ghost makes?
A: A boo-boo.

Q: What sound does a chicken's ghost make?
A: "Peck-a-boo."

Q: Who's the most famous barber on Elm Street?
A: Freddy Crew-cut. (But watch out! He cuts hair with his glove. . . .)

Q: What's the difference between an adult and a noisy ghost?
A: One is all grown, the other is all groan.

"Say," said the Wolfman, "I hear the Frankenstein Monster moved to be nearer to a city."

"That's right," said the Mummy.

"Which city did he move near?"

The Mummy grumbled, "Electricity."

"I hear the Frankenstein Monster also got married," said the Wolfman. "Why did he do that?"

The Mummy muttered, "Because he found a woman, and they fell in love with each shudder."

Q: What's the difference between Dracula and a mosquito waiting behind him?
A: One bites necks, the other bites next.

"Bet I can make a witch scratch herself," Nellie said to Telly.

"How?"

"Simple! By taking away her 'w.' "

Q: What's a skeleton's favorite instrument?
A: The trom-bone.

Q: What do you call a zombie who's only an inch tall?
A: Tomb Thumb.

Q: Why did Godzilla wrap a very long string around the Japanese city?
A: He wanted to play with a Tokyo-yo

Q: What do you call a monster whale with a large vocabulary?
A: Moby Dick-tionary.

Q: Why is the Mississippi River like a monster from Neptune?
A: They both have five eyes.

Q: What's the difference between a group of zombies and a sock that's been darned?
A: One is dead men, the other is mended.

Q: What kind of sailors plunder the high seas
. . . but only after sundown?
A: Vampirates.

Q: Why was Dr. Frankenstein never lonely?
A: Because he could always make friends.

Q: What do you call a zombie who becomes
your pal?
A: A ghoul-friend.

"Did you hear what happened at the Wolfman's party?" the Black Lagoon Creature
asked the Metaluna Mutant.

"No, what?"

"The Wolfman ate everyone at the table!"

"Why?"

The Creature said, "Because someone told
him that when he blows out the candles on
his cake, he should get birthday vicious."

Q: What's King Kong's favorite kind of cookie?
A: Chocolate chimp.

Q: What's Dracula's favorite kind of ice-cream topping?
A: Blooderscotch.

Q: What's the Wolfman's favorite breakfast food?
A: Fur-ina.

Q: What monster wears a mask and is big and gray?
A: The Elephantom of the Opera.

Q: What do monsters always order in fast-food restaurants?
A: French frights.

Q: What do ghosts order there?
A: Ham-boo-gers.

Q: What do werewolves order there?
A: Cheeseburg*rrrrrr*s.

Q: What do banshees order there?
A: A milk shriek.

Q: What do you call a dragon's bad dream?
A: A knightmare.

Q: What do ghosts wear when it snows?
A: Boooooots.

Q: How fast can a werewolf run?
A: Sixty mauls-an-hour.

Q: What is the one room ghosts avoid when haunting a house?
A: The living room.

LAW AND ORDER

A prisoner walked over to his new cellmate and asked, "What are you in for?"

The new man answered, "I was driving my car too slow."

"Too slow?" the other prisoner said. "Don't you mean too *fast*?"

"No, too slow. The police caught me!"

Another prisoner asked his cellmate, "Do you know the least dangerous kind of robbery to commit?"

"No," said the other. "What?"

"A safe robbery."

The police-academy instructor said to her student, "Jenkins! What would you do if you saw a kidnapping?"

After thinking a moment, Cadet Jenkins replied, "I'd wake him up."

Q: What did the robber do to escape from the police?
A: He stepped on a scale and got a weigh.

"I can't believe it," Moe said to his friend Irv. "My wallet was stolen right from under my nose!"

"Gee," said Irv, "it probably would have been safer in your pants pocket."

Q: What's the difference between a court of law and a tray of frozen water?
A: In one you get justice, in the other you get just ice.

Q: What's the difference between gunslingers and sky divers?
A: One has a shoot-out, the other has a chute-out.

After breaking out of jail, Jake and Zeke had to cross a river. As they did so, Zeke tossed a penny into the water and watched it float away.

"Why'd ya do that?" asked Jake.

"So that when the bloodhounds get here, they follow the cent."

The warden said to the criminal, "For being so rude, I'm going to put you on a diet of bread and water. How do you like it?"

The criminal thought for a second, then answered, "Whole wheat toast and Perrier."

The police officer said to Mad Mel, "Why did you punch the dentist?"

"Because he got on my nerves!"

Three boys were brought before the judge after causing a ruckus at the zoo.

"Who are you, and what did you do?" the judge asked the first boy."

"I'm Clark, and I threw peanuts to the elephants."

The judge looked at the second boy. "Who are you, and what did you do?"

"I'm Robert, and I threw peanuts to the elephants."

The judge looked at the third boy, who was all bloody and bruised. "Who are you, and what did you do?"

"I'm Peanuts."

"Excuse me," the police officer said to the woman in the street, "but we're looking for a man with a baby buggy."

"I see," she said. "Wouldn't it be better to use a police car instead?"

Q: What is the name of the biggest horse thief of all time?

A: Al Capony.

"Sir," said the police officer, "I regret to inform you that your dog has been chasing a man on a bicycle."

"That's crazy," said the man. "My dog doesn't know how to ride a bicycle."

Q: What is a law officer's favorite board game?
A: Monopolice.

"All right," said the forest warden, "who saw which of these men cut down this rare tree?"

A camper replied, "Only the chain saw."

"My dad's in jail for opening a bakery," said Hugh.

"Really? Since when is that a crime?"

"Since he opened it with a crowbar."

"I'm afraid I'm going to have to lock you up," the police officer said to Machinegun Milton.

"What's the charge?" demanded Milton.

"No charge. It's free!"

Later on, the judge said to Milton, "The court can produce at least a dozen witnesses who saw you walk into the bank and rob it."

"Big deal!" said Machinegun. "I can bring in billions of people who didn't see a thing!"

Naturally, a lot of Machinegun Milton's friends showed up at his trial. And every time the judge said something, the robber's friends would boo and hiss.

"All right," the judge said at last. "The next person who makes a peep will be thrown into the street!"

At that point, Milton stood and yelled, "Peep!"

Bert and Ernie were brought before the judge.

"I understand you were fighting," said the judge.

"I had no choice!" said Bert. "Ernie started it—he bit off a piece of my finger!"

"Nevertheless," said the judge. "I'm fining you *both* two hundred dollars. And I expect you, Ernie, to keep the peace for at least one year!"

"I can't, your honor," said Ernie.

"Why not?"

"I already spit it out!"

When Bert got home, his wife asked, "How did you make out in court?"

Bert answered, "Fine."

The man ran into the detective's office, jumped on the man's head, and said, "One, two, three, four—"

The detective immediately pushed the man off.

"What do you think you're doing?"

"I'm in trouble," said the man, "and someone told me I could count on you!"

The criminal was surprised to find one of his gang members cutting the legs off beds in their hideout.

"What are you doing?" the leader asked.

"Just what you told me to," said the gang member. "You said we were going to have to lie low for a while."

Q: Who's the fastest criminal on two wheels?
A: A motor-psycho.

MOVIES AND TV

Q: What's small, blue, and cracks jokes?
A: Eddie Smurfy.

Q: What is a witch's favorite movie?
A: *Star Warts.* They think it's hex-cellant!

Q: What is a witch's second-favorite movie?
A: *Gone With the Wand.* It leaves them spell-
bound!

108

The Dingle family was watching *Star Trek*.

"You know," said young Swoosie Dingle, "Mr. Spock has funny ears, but Captain Kirk's ears are even stranger."

"Why do you say that?" asked her mother.

"Because he has three of them. A left ear, a right ear, and a final front ear."

Q: What's the favorite TV program in hives around the nation?
A: "The Cos-bee Show."

Q: What's a bee's second-favorite TV show?
A: "Saturday Night Hive."

Q: What's the favorite TV program in little bug colonies around the nation?
A: "Rose-ant."

Q: What's the favorite TV program among cows?
A: "Herd of the Class."

Q: Why aren't there any movie theaters in the jungle?
A: No one likes the lions outside.

The actor turned to a woman sitting beside him at the theater.

"Perhaps you've seen me," he said. "I was in the movie *Diner*."

"Did you have a big role?"

"No. Just a muffin and coffee."

"It's a fact," said Will. "Watching TV causes violent behavior."

"What makes you say that?" asked his friend.

Will said, "Every time I turn it on, my mom has a fit!"

Q: What famous American filmmaker lived in a safe?

A: Vault Disney.

Q: What are they calling the new cable-TV channel which is all about good things to eat?

A: Mmmmm-TV.

Q: What cable channel should you watch with a can of room freshener nearby?

A: H-BO.

Q: What incredible invention not only tapes TV shows, but eats ants that come into the house?

A: A VCaardvark

Q: What did they call MTV when all the VJs went out on strike?

A: Empty-V.

Q: What animals appear on every TV channel at six o'clock each night?

A: The evening gnus.

Q: What's a postal carrier's favorite monster movie?

A: *Mailiens.*

PARENTS

One kid said to the other. "My dad is so cheap, there's only one thing he'll ever part with."

"What's that?" asked his friend.

Said the first boy: "A comb."

Ethel said to Frances, "Why is your husband pacing like that?"

"He's worried about our teenage son," Frances replied.

"Oh, really? What does your son have?"

"His driver's license."

When his father came home from his first day of cleaning chimneys, John asked, "Dad, how did you like your first day on the job?"

"Oh," said his father, "it soots me."

"How's business?" the girl asked her father, the tailor.

"Sew-sew," her dad replied.

"How's business?" the boy asked his mother, an astronomer.

"It's looking up," she replied.

"How's business?" the girl asked her mother, an author.

"It's all write," she answered.

"These bills are so high!" wailed Mr. Howland. "I'd be happy if just one thing went down."

"Dad—have a look at my report card.

The father complained to his neighbor, "Every time my daughter needs money, she says, 'Hi, handsome—' "

"Hi, handsome?"

"Yes. 'Hi, handsome over!' "

Elizabeth answered the door.

"Dad, there's a gentleman here collecting for the new pool in the park."

"All right," said Elizabeth's father, "give him a pail of water."

Q: Why don't parents ever believe what their kids tell them from bed?

A: Because the kids are lying.

Speaking of bed, one child asked her father, "Daddy—why do I have to go to bed?"

He smiled and answered, "Because the bed won't come to you."

SOLDIERS

Q: What is a sergeant's favorite month?
A: March.

Marching in front of his men, the sergeant decided to find out if Private Hargrove was really the dumbest man in the service.

"See here," said the sergeant. "What would happen if you were in a battle and one of your ears was shot off?"

"Well, sir," said the private, "I wouldn't be able to hear out of that side."

"Correct. Now tell me: what would happen if both of your ears were shot off?"

"That's easy, sir," said the private. "Then I wouldn't be able to see."

The sergeant glared at Private Hargrove.

"What kind of nonsense is that? Why wouldn't you be able to see?"

"Because, sir. If both of my ears were shot off, my helmet would slip over my eyes!"

The sergeant placed the prisoner in front of the firing squad and asked the doomed man, "Do you have any last requests?"

"Just one," said the man. "I'd like to sing a song."

"Very well," said the sergeant.

Clearing his throat, the prisoner sang, "One billion bottles of Coke on the wall, one billion bottles of Coke. . . ."

"Did you hear?" pilot Jenkins shouted as he ran into the hangar, "Captain Smith fell out of a B-1 bomber, without a parachute, and he wasn't even hurt!"

"That's impossible!" said the other pilot. "The fall would have killed him."

Jenkins shook his head. "The bomber hadn't taken off yet."

Q: What did one retired admiral say to the other retired admiral?
A: "Long time, no sea!"

Q: Which month does a soldier hate most of all?
A: March.

Then there was the baby who crawled to an army post because she thought she could join the infantry. . . .

Q: What kind of explosive makes no noise?
A: A mime bomb.

Q: What's green and goes "boom!"?
A: A lime bomb.

Q: What costs ten cents and explodes?
A: A dime bomb.

Q: What goes, "Gloom, doom, *boom*"?
A: A rhyme bomb.

Q: What's the difference between an aged military police officer and a hundred-year-old man?
A: One's an old sentry, the other's a century old.

SPORTS

Q: How do baseball pitchers celebrate New Year's?

A: They throw a party.

It was a warm summer's afternoon when Jim picked up his girlfriend to go to the baseball game. Much to his surprise, she came out wearing three sweaters, mittens, and a scarf, and a wool hat.

"Judy, why are you wearing all those things? It's ninety degrees!"

"But it'll be cold at the stadium," she replied as she got in the car. "You said so."

"I did?"

"Yes," she said. "You said there were going to be eighty thousand fans there!"

Q: Why does a baseball pitcher lift one leg
   when he throws?
A: Because he'd fall if he lifted them both

Mrs. Kaplan was amused when her five-
year-old son Aaron gave his baby brother Jay
baseball cards for his birthday.

"It was very thoughtful of you to give Jay
those cards," she said, "but there's a problem: he can't read."

"That's okay, Mom," said Aaron. "He can
still look at the pitchers."

Q: Why did the football coach send in second
   string players?
A: He wanted to tie the game.

Q: Who's the only person that's played for
   every team in the National Hockey League?
A: The organist.

Leroy decided to go fishing, and ignoring the "No Fishing" sign at his favorite lake, he cast his line and sat down on the bank.

After a few minutes, the game warden walked over.

"Mister, didn't you see the sign here?" the warden asked. "The one that says 'No Fishing'?"

"I did," said Leroy, "but I'm not fishing."

"Oh? Then what *are* you doing?"

Leroy answered, "I'm drowning worms."

Q: Why did they stop selling soda at the doubleheader?
A: The home team lost the opener.

Q: What's a cheerleader's favorite beverage?
A: Root beer.

At the football game, Mitch stood in a long line to get sodas.

When he returned to his seat, he asked his girlfriend. "What's the score?"

"Nine to three," she said.

"Who's winning?"

"The team with nine," the young woman replied.

Q: Why are losing teams always so hot?
A: Because they have the fewest fans.

Q: How is the ocean like a football game that goes into overtime?
A: One is tidal, the other is all-tied.

"Did you hear about the baseball game that was played in the fog?" one sports nut asked another.

"Really. Did anybody hit a ball?"

"Nope. Just mist."

Q: How would you describe a five-hundred-pound hockey player?

A: As someone who's worth his weight in goals.

Just before the marathon, Arthur was surprised to find runner Murray holding his sneakers under the faucet in the kitchen.

"Why are you doing that?" Murray asked.

Arthur said, "I figured it would help if I washed them in running water."

Q: What's the difference between a New York baseball fan and a dentist?

A: One is a Yank rooter, the other is a root yanker.

"Of course God's a baseball fan," Michael said to Bernard. "It says so in the Bible."

"Where does it say that?" Bernard asked.

"At the very start, when it says, 'In the big inning . . .' "

Q: What does a baseball player wear when he gets really old?

A: Out.

Q: Why is basketball the most disgusting sport?

A: Because the players spend half their time dribbling all over the court.

"Did you hear about the teachers' hockey game?" Bud said to Bub.

"No, what happened?"

"No one moved for all three periods."

"Why?"

"Because the puck was so dumb, the teachers refused to pass it!"

Q: What is a basketball player's favorite kind of book?

A: A collection of tall tales.

Q: What's the difference between a thief and an umpire?
A: One steals watches, the other watches steals.

Q: What is an executioner's favorite sport?
A: Hang gliding.

"Pop!" said the teenager, "I won the broad jump at the high school."

"That's terrific," said the man, "but I thought you'd entered the shot put."

"I did," replied the boy. "But as I was about to throw, I backed into a javelin."

Q: What did the marathoner feel after losing the long, long race?
A: She felt the agony of de feet.

Remember Leroy, the guy who ignored the "No Fishing" sign a few jokes back?

Well, after the warden chased him from that watering hole, Leroy went to another. He ignored the sign there and settled down. Before long, the game warden found him.

"What are you doing *now*?" the warden asked. "The sign here says 'No Fishing Allowed.' "

"I'm not," said Leroy. "I'm being very, very quiet."

"Let me see your permit," the game warden said to Leroy. "You can't fish without one."

"I don't need one," said the fisher. "I'm doing fine with worms."

Actually, the game warden couldn't understand why anyone would want to go fishing in the first place. As he often told his wife, "Fishing is when the jerk on one end of the line waits for a jerk on the other end."

Q: What becomes more difficult to catch the faster you run?
A: Your breath.

Tom asked Tim, "What's the quietest sport in the world?"
"I would say fishing."
"Wrong," said Tom. "It's bowling."
"Bowling?"
"Sure! You can always hear a pin drop."

Cornelius said to Bubba, "Your mother and father must be weight lifters."
"Why do you say that?"
Cornelius answered, "How else could they raise a big dumbbell like you?"

Q: What's the difference between a marathoner and a commuter?
A: One trains for runs, the other runs for trains.

"Ma," said Julius, "I don't want to play football with my little brother."

"Why not?" asked the mother.

"Because I can't kick him as far as a real ball!"

Q: Why do great bowlers always get strikes?
A: Because they have no time to spare.

Janice and Janet were playing golf when a bird flew overhead.

"Look at that lovely swan!" said Janice.

"It's a duck," corrected Janet.

"Swan," said Janice.

"Duck!"

"Swan!"

Just then, Janet saw someone slice a golf ball in their direction.

"Duck!" shouted Janet.

"Swan!" screamed Janice.

"Ka-*bonk*!" went the golf ball.

Q: Why don't artists take up boxing?
A: Because the fights would end in a draw.

Q: Why did Cinderella's team lose the soccer game?
A: Because once again, she ran from the ball. . . .

"Did you hear about the boxer who couldn' start a fire?" Bugs said to Elmer.
"No. Why?"
"Because he lost all his matches."

Q: What's the difference between Prince Charles and a football?
A: One is heir to the throne, the other is throne to the air.

At the bell, the bloodied boxer staggered into the corner.

"Hey!" snarled his manager. "I thought you were going to go out there and show him what you're made of!"

"I did," gasped the boxer. "He knocked the stuffing out of me!"

Q: When a three-hundred-fifty-pound wrestler breaks his toe in the ring, what's the best way to get back to the locker room?
A: With a toe truck.

"Did you hear about the diver who leaped into a glass of Pepsi?" Doug asked Judy.

"No! How many bones did she break?"

"None," Doug replied. "It was a soft drink."

Q: What's the best time of year to use a trampoline?
A: Springtime.

Billy sighed, "I wish I had the money to buy a million baseballs."

His pal Dickie said, "What would you do with a million baseballs?"

"Nothing," said Billy. "I just wish I had that much money."

Q: What nationality does the best in a bicycle race?
A: Someone who's rushin'.

Q: What nationality does the winner of a bicycle race automatically become?
A: Finnish.

"Uncle Ted," said little Todd as he ran toward the beach, "I was standing on the shore and I saw a tuna fish."

"Really?" said Uncle Ted. "How was the tuna holding the rod?"

An old woman walked into the sport-supply store.

"I'd like a baseball bat for my grandson," she told the clerk.

"Sorry," he said, "we sell bats, we don't trade them."

The man ran into the fishing store.

"Hurry!" he said. "I have to catch the ferry, and I need some bait!"

The clerk scratched his head. "Gee, mister . . . I don't have any bait that a ferry would like."

While watching a man water-ski, little Eva said to her father, "That man is so silly! He's never going to be able to catch that boat!"

After riding a huge wave, a surfer ran onto the beach.

"Holy moley," said a young boy who was watching him, "you sure are good!"

"Well," smiled the teenager, "I've been surfing since I was six."

"Wow!" said the boy. "You must be tired, too!"

Q: Who's the nuttiest baseball player of all time?
A: Mickey Mental.

Q: Who's the funniest football player of all time?
A: Joke Namath—quarterback for the New York Jests.

Keith and Richard were watching the basketball game when Keith suddenly jumped to his feet and screamed, "That ball was a tired kangaroo!"

Richard asked, "Why did you call that ball a tired kangaroo?"

"Because it was out of bounds!"

Speedy Spencer was the fastest runner in the school, and Mildred was tired of hearing him brag about it. One day, she approached him in the corridor.

"I'll bet ten dollars," she said, "that if you give me a two-foot head start, I can beat you in a race."

Spencer laughed and said, "You're on."

They both gave ten dollars to another student to hold, then agreed to have the race after school.

When Spencer saw Mildred, he threw up his hands and forfeited the race.

She was standing two feet up on a ladder.

Q: What kind of drawing did Babe Ruth do in the bullpen?
A: A Yankee Doodle.

Q: What do you call a football player who fails at playing quarterback, halfback, and fullback?
A: A drawback.

The two baseball fans were watching the Dodgers lose. Suddenly the announcer said, "A new Dodgers pitcher is coming into the game."

One of the fans said, "Phew! Now that's a relief!"

"Know what the national sport is in Spain?" Percy asked Irwin. "It's bullfighting. And in England it's cricket."

"Hmmm," said Irwin. "I'd rather live in England."

"Why?"

"Because I'd rather fight a cricket."

Mort asked Gene, "Why are you taking your math homework to your aerobics class?"

Gene said, "I have to reduce some fractions."

"Did you hear about poor Juan?" Carlos asked his friend. "He was killed on the golf course."

"No! How did it happen?"

"A flying golf ball went right through his head."

"How terrible!" said the friend. "A hole in Juan."

Q: What's the difference between a boxer and a boy with a cold?
A: One knows his blows, the other blows his nose.

Q: What's the difference between a crowd at a bullfight and a farmer begging his chicken for eggs?
A: One shouts, "Olé!" and the other shouts, "Oh, lay!"

Q: What did the right soccer shoe say to the left soccer shoe?
A: "Between us, we'll have a ball!"

"It's incredible!" Ralph said to his friend. "I saw a coach go by . . . and it didn't have any wheels!"

"How can that be?" said the friend.

"It was my football coach."

AND FINALLY:
YUCCH!
SOME REALLY DISGUSTING JOKES ABOUT
JIMMY THE BUG-EATER!

Sal asked, "Did you hear about Jimmy, the new kid in school? He does bird impressions."

"No, really?"

"Yes," said Sal. "He eats worms."

Mary looked at Jimmy's plate at lunchtime. It was covered with long, stringy things.

"Ewwww," said Mary, "what's that?"

Jimmy mumbled something.

"Did you say spaghetti?" Mary asked. "That looks like worms!"

"It is worms," Jimmy said, slurping up a strand. "I said it's bug-hetti."

Mary turned green, but she couldn't help noticing he had a side dish. It was square, covered with tomato sauce . . . and had brown things sticking from the sides.

"Wh-what's that?" she asked.

"What's it look like?"

"Lasagna."

"You're close," said Jimmy. "It's tarantu-lasagna."

Q: When Jimmy is at home, what does he love to spread on bread?

A: Peanut butterfly.

Q: If there's no peanut butterfly around, what will Jimmy make himself for lunch?

A: He'll get some bread, go outside, and make himself an antwich.

Q: What do you think Jimmy's favorite dessert is? (Hint: it has squiggly, chewy things in it!)

A: Lice cream.

Q: What's his second-favorite dessert? (Hint: it has dark, squooshy things in it!)
A: Fly's cream.

Q: If none of that's around, what flavor custard will Jimmy eat instead?
A: Locust-ard.

Q: What does he use to wash his food down?
A: Lemon-gnat or fruit-fly punch.

Q: What's the best way to describe Jimmy's diet?
A: Moth-watering.

Q: Jimmy's also thinking of writing a cookbook. What do you think it will contain?
A: All his favorite recip-bees.